PAUL HENRY

Paul Henry
1876–1958

S B KENNEDY

PAUL HENRY

Paul Henry
1876–1958

S B KENNEDY

TOWN HOUSE, DUBLIN
IN ASSOCIATION WITH
THE NATIONAL GALLERY OF IRELAND

Published in 1991 by

Town House

41 Marlborough Road

Donnybrook

Dublin 4

in association with The National Gallery of Ireland

British Library Cataloguing in Publication Data

Kennedy, S. B.

Paul Henry—(Lives of Irish artists)

1. Ireland. Paintings

I. Title II. National Gallery of Ireland III. Series

759.2915

ISBN: 0-948524-22-7

Cover: *Lakeside Cottages* (1923–32)
Title page: Portrait by Grace Henry (Ulster Museum)

Managing editor: Treasa Coady

Series editor: Brian P Kennedy (NGI)

Text editor: Elaine Campion

Design concept: Q Design

Typeset by Printset & Design Ltd, Dublin

Printed in Italy

CONTENTS

PAUL HENRY

Dr S B Kennedy was born in Belfast. He studied art at the Belfast College of Art and later read art history at the Open University and Trinity College, Dublin. In 1987 he was an Honorary Research Fellow at the Institute of Irish Studies, Queen's University, Belfast. He is presently Curator of Twentieth-Century Art at the Ulster Museum, Belfast.

Any observer of Irish art in the twentieth century will notice the prominence of landscape painting and especially of scenes of the west of Ireland. From the turn of the century until the late 1950s, landscape played a particularly central role in the development of Irish art, for many reasons. Artists approached the landscape from various points of view, but almost without exception, all were influenced to some degree by the work of Paul Henry, RHA.

CHILDHOOD IN BELFAST

Paul Henry was born in Belfast in 1876, the third of four sons of the Revd R M Henry, a Protestant fundamentalist, and his wife Kate Ann (née Berry). Life in the Henry household was organised according to a strict pattern of parental discipline. Yet, despite his youthful rebellion against this, in later life Paul Henry came to admire his parents, especially his father for his enquiring mind, his sense of purpose, and his devotion to duty. In June 1891 the Revd Henry died, and Paul, who was still a schoolboy, felt his loss deeply. At this time he read Henry Thoreau's *Walden*, a tale of solitary life near Concord, Massachusetts, which was to have a lasting influence on his outlook. He also developed an interest in art and began to take lessons from the artist Thomas Bond Walker. On leaving school, in 1893, Paul was apprenticed briefly as a designer with a Belfast linen firm, before enrolling as a student at the Belfast Government School of Art. There, he soon made his mark, and was advised to move on to one of the London art schools. He was accepted for a place at the Herkomer School of Art at Bushey, but financial difficulties prevented him from attending. His cousin John Henry MacFarland heard about his disappointment and volunteered to pay for his studies. In 1898, Paul went, not to London but to Paris, then the mecca of the art world. Thus began the first great adventure of his life.

❧

A Student in Paris

In Paris, Paul settled into the bohemian world of the Latin quarter. He affected a radical change in his dress, wearing his hair long, a bow-tie loosely tied, and a wide-brimmed hat (the latter being an affectation of dress he kept for the rest of his life). It was here that he first encountered avant-garde painting, and he was especially impressed by the work of Van Gogh. 'I would have walked half across Paris to look at a new thing by him,' he wrote years later. He took a studio in the Rue de la Grande Chaumière and attended classes at the famous Académie Julian. But when Whistler, then at the height of his notoriety, opened his Académie Carmen, he quickly enrolled there. Under Whistler he learned to modulate close tonal relationships and to emphasise the underlying abstract qualities of his compositions.

This was to be the most carefree period of Henry's life. He met and became friendly with Grace Mitchell, a fellow-painter from St Fergus, near Aberdeen, and, despite having little contact with home, from time to time he met a number of compatriots, including Edith Somerville and Violet Ross, Constance Gore Booth, W B Yeats and John *11* Synge.

He began to work in charcoal, a medium with which he always felt comfortable, and occasionally he went into the countryside beyond the city to make studies of the landscape. He remained in Paris for about two years, and they were the most formative years of his career. But by 1900 his funds were running low and he had to start thinking of earning his living. Somewhat reluctantly he made his way to London, hoping to secure employment as an illustrator on a newspaper, magazine or journal.

☙

AT WORK IN LONDON

If Paris was a city of dreams for Paul Henry, London was a city of realities. Finding work as an illustrator proved to

12

be more difficult that he had anticipated. Day after day he trudged round Fleet Street with his work, often without success. But he was persistent, and after a time he got a few commissions to design book jackets and other similar jobs. He met up with some old friends from Belfast, including Robert Lynd who was living in London and making his way in journalism. Another friendship renewed in these years was with Ladbroke Black, editor of the *Morning Leader*, who had encouraged him while he was in Paris to write about life in the studios and cafés. He also met Frank Rutter, the editor of the weekly *Today*. In time Rutter commissioned him to produce black and white illustrations for his paper, and these provided his first regular income.

Paul Henry's earliest extant work dates from this period, that is, from about 1900 or 1901. As an illustrator his subject matter depended upon the stories he was asked to depict—often romances. His medium was almost invariably charcoal, and influenced by Whistler he used it with great subtlety to emphasise mood and atmosphere, often contriving a sense of mystery. His technique was partly determined by the needs of contemporary reproduction techniques. Slowly Henry began to carve a niche for himself and, in the years which followed, he made illustrations for *Today*, *The Graphic*, *Black and White* and other journals, as well as for a number of books.

cont. p25

ILLUSTRATIONS

PLATE 1

Water Meadows 1908–10

Pl 1   **B**efore settling in Ireland, Henry lived for a time near Guildford in Surrey. There was a small area of bogland near his home, which held a strange fascination for him. 'I was happier there than in any other part of the country,' he later wrote. Even in this early work one can see the prominence which he was always to give to the sky and cloud formations, and the emphasis on the mood and atmosphere of the landscape.

Charcoal and white on paper; 34 x 46.5 cm
Ulster Museum, Belfast

PLATE 2

The Potato Diggers 1912

14

Pl 2 **O**ne *of Henry's few dated paintings, done shortly after he settled on Achill. He usually made such compositions in the studio, from drawings done out of doors. Observing the islanders was difficult for, as he said, they distrusted 'the sketcher', believing that in drawing them he was taking something from them. Henry's early Achill pictures have a feeling of monumentality. The red petticoats were almost universally worn by the peasantry in the west of Ireland in Henry's time.*

Oil on canvas; 51 x 46 cm
National Gallery of Ireland

PLATE 3
_____

Boy on a Donkey going for Turf 1910-13

Pl 3   T*his canvas, which sparkles with vitality of concept and execution, probably dates from Henry's first visit to Achill. The semi-impressionist handling of the paint*   15 *provokes a sense of spontaneity which contrasts with the unhurried life of the islander. There were few roads on Achill then and nearly everything had to be transported in creels on the backs of donkeys.*

Oil on canvas; 12.4 x 14.9 cm
National Gallery of Ireland

PLATE 4

Launching the Currach 1910–11

16

Pl 4   F*ish formed a large part of the diet on Achill. The currach, carried by two or three men, required no harbours and was the ideal craft for local use. For such an early work, Henry's range of colours is unusually bright and the subject matter, too, is different. The energy*

and anticipation of the moment are caught in the contrast between the dark mass of the figures and the light background.

Oil on canvas; 41 x 60 cm
National Gallery of Ireland

PLATE 5

Old People Watching a Dance 1910-11

18

Pl 5

This composition was almost certainly made from sketches done surreptitiously, for the islanders would not willingly sit for their portraits. Henry disliked having to work in such a manner but had no option and, besides, he found the elderly people of the island to be especially interesting, admiring their sturdiness of character and dignity of manner. He felt that they represented the end of an epoch, 'the slow fading out of an era'.

Oil on board; 29.9 x 29.2 cm
Private collection

PLATE 6

Connemara Landscape 1913

Pl 6   **A**n early example of Henry's concern for stillness, for
the other-worldliness he associated with the landscape of
the west of Ireland. From this time, human figures became
less important to his compositions and he emphasised the
monumentality of the landscape. Paradoxically, in scenes
such as this, one is constantly aware of human presence,
of the universality of our attachment to 'place'. Henry's
ability to render such qualities gives his work a lasting
importance.

19

Oil on canvas; 67 x 79 cm
Private collection

PLATE 7

Grand Canal Dock, Ringsend, Dublin *c* 1920-9

20

Pl 7   This drawing illustrates Henry's continued use of charcoal, to which he had been introduced during his student days. 'No chalk or crayon has the same soft, velvety quality,' he later noted. The subject matter, an industrial landscape, is unusual for Henry, but he has treated it in the same concise manner which characterises his better known landscapes. The emphasis on atmosphere illustrates Whistler's continuing influence.

Charcoal on paper; 40 x 33.2 cm
National Gallery of Ireland

PLATE 8

Dawn, Killary Harbour 1922-3

Pl 8   *In this painting there are no people, yet there is a redolence of humanity; a strong sense of early morning light and atmosphere; and, in the simple massing of forms and almost monochromatic palette, an emphasis on abstraction underpinning the composition. The latter* 21 *quality demonstrates the influence of Whistler, which remained with Henry throughout his career. This rendering of Killary Harbour, a fiord-like inlet in Connemara, is one of Henry's finest 'pure' landscapes.*

Oil on canvas; 69.1 x 83.3 cm
Ulster Museum, Belfast

PLATE 9

Lakeside Cottages *c* 1923–32

22

Pl 9   **W**ith the purchase in 1922 of one of his landscapes by the Luxembourg Gallery in Paris, Henry was regarded as one of Ireland's most influential painters. This composition shows him at the height of his powers; it is the quintessential 'Paul Henry'. His style, use of colour

and sense of scale are perfectly matched to the rugged countryside. He has painted not just a scene, but a way of life, and one which has almost disappeared.

Oil on canvas; 40 x 60 cm
Hugh Lane Municipal Gallery of Modern Art, Dublin

PLATE 10

Peat Ditches, Ireland 1934

24

Pl 10 **T**his picture was almost certainly painted *i*
September–October 1934, during Henry's first visit to th
Dingle peninsula. While his approach to composition h*e*
changed little from his earlier years, his use of colour
richer and lends a more luscious feel to the landscap*e*
Gone is the emphasis on surface texture; the landscap*e*
has now become 'symbolically Irish'.

Oil on canvas; 30.5 x 40.6 cm
Private collection

(Photo courtesy of Pyms Gallery, London)

cont. from p12

But Henry found such work tedious and, as befitted his training in Paris, he began to turn towards pictures. In 1906 he exhibited for the first time, showing four pictures, which were almost certainly charcoal drawings, at a group exhibition in the Goupil Gallery in London. From then on, he became a regular exhibitor there and elsewhere.

In 1908, along with Frank Rutter and others, Henry helped to found the Allied Artists' Association, an independent forum for progressive artists, and he exhibited at the Association's first exhibition, in the Albert Hall, London, in July of that year. On that occasion he showed landscapes, namely *The Shower*, *Storm Clouds* and *West Wind*, titles suggestive of the mood and atmosphere which was to characterise his later work. Among the visitors to the exhibition were Hugh Lane and Dermod O'Brien. They were impressed by Henry's work and suggested that he should exhibit at the Royal Hibernian Academy, which he did for the first time in 1910.

During his early years in London Henry's friendship with Grace Mitchell blossomed and they married in September 1903. For a time the Henrys shared lodgings near Guildford, Surrey, with Robert Lynd. In 1909 Lynd married the writer Sylvia Dryhurst and they went to Achill Island, off the Connemara coast, for their honeymoon. On his return to London, Lynd spoke so enthusiastically of the island and its people that Paul, who had read Synge's *Riders to the Sea* and was curious about the west, decided to see it for himself, and so he and Grace went there for a fortnight's holiday in the summer of 1910.

ॐ

A PAINTER ON ACHILL 1910–19

Paul Henry's maternal grandfather had been a clergyman on Achill, so talk of the island can hardly have been completely novel to him. The Henrys were so enthralled by Achill that, instead of returning to London after a fortnight, they stayed for almost a year, and later, in 1912, they settled there. Paul said that he felt he had been carried to Achill 'on the currents of life'.

While he had lived in Surrey, Paul's routine had been to spend one or two afternoons a week in London visiting editors and others for whom he had work, and to paint in his spare time. There was a small area of bogland near where he lived, which had a particular fascination for him, and he sketched it a number of times. *Water Meadows* (*Pl 1*), a charcoal drawing, was probably done here. The scene is similar to many in the west of Ireland, and it is not surprising that he later felt so much at home on the island.

On Achill Paul Henry found the subject matter he had subconsciously been seeking. The people there, wringing out a meagre existence against great odds, reminded him of the peasants in pictures by the well-known French artist Jean François Millet. Millet's influence can be seen in a number of paintings done shortly after Henry's first visit to Achill. Of these, the *Potato Diggers* (*Pl 2*) is a good example. The composition is concise, and the figure bent with outstretched arm is clearly a quotation from Millet's *The Gleaners* (Louvre). The dress and gait of the figures convey clearly the plight of such people, and evoke feelings of pathos.

Figures predominate in most of Henry's early Achill paintings. He depicted all aspects of life there; the islanders at work in the fields; fetching turf (*Pl 3*); harvesting seaweed; preparing to go fishing, as in *Launching the Currach* (*Pl 4*); checking the catch in *The Lobster Pots* (1911–13); and relaxing in the evening, as in *Old People Watching a Dance* (*Pl 5*). The assurance and fluidity of his brushwork in these pictures are indicative of his vitality and enjoyment of life.

In 1911 Henry first showed pictures of Achill, in Belfast, and from then on he exhibited almost annually there and in Dublin. These exhibitions provided a meagre living, but sufficient to enable him to paint full time, as life in Achill was inexpensive. A measure of his prominence at the time was the inclusion of three of his pictures in the exhibition of Irish art at the Whitechapel Art Gallery, London, in 1913.

Although Henry had occasionally painted landscapes

devoid of people, as, for example, in *Clare Island from Achill* (1910–11) and *The Lake of the Tears of the Sorrowing Women* (Sligo Art Gallery), from about 1913 people became less important to his compositions and the landscape itself took priority. He began to travel more widely in County Mayo. He often rose at dawn to observe the landscape in the stillness of the early morning, and he was fascinated by what he once termed the 'other worldliness' of the Irish landscape at that hour. This quality can be seen clearly in *Connemara Landscape* (*Pl 6*), painted in 1913. It is one of his few dated pictures and thus indicates the development of his technique. Although these landscapes are devoid of people, they remain redolent of humanity and of the struggle for survival in a harsh environment. This line of development culminated in about 1922–3 in *Dawn, Killary Harbour* (*Pl 8*). Here the influence of Whistler, his teacher, is evident in the finely balanced tones, the limited palette and abstraction of the composition. Paul Henry also suffered from a mild form of colour blindness and this, too, probably influenced his manipulation of tonal relationships.

While Paul was happy on Achill, his wife Grace disliked the conditions there. She had been brought up in well-to-do surroundings and no doubt longed for more comfort and society than Achill could offer. From about 1916 their marriage began to deteriorate, although following their move to Dublin in 1919 they were for a time more settled.

ॐ

THE DUBLIN YEARS, 1919-30

Shortly after his arrival in Dublin, Paul Henry took a studio at No. 13A Merrion Row, which was to be his base until 1930. The early 1920s—a momentous period in Irish history—brought him increased recognition. He and Grace continued to exhibit together regularly. Paul also became involved in the Dublin art scene, and in the summer of 1920, to promote avant-garde painting in the face of hostility from officialdom, he and Grace, along with some others, including Clare Marsh, Jack B Yeats, Letitia Hamilton, James Sleator and Mary Swanzy, founded the Society of Dublin Painters. Based in rooms at No. 7 St Stephen's Green, the Dublin Painters represented all that was progressive in Irish art and, until the foundation of the Irish Exhibition of Living Art in 1943, they kept alight the torch of the avant-garde. Henry had little to do with the Society after the mid-1920s, but it continued to prosper until the 1950s.

By the early 1920s Paul Henry's technique was assured, and for the rest of his career his style changed little. His compositions are characterised by a few boldly juxtaposed elements, with great emphasis given to the sky and cloud formations. Yet, as many of his imitators have discovered, his images are deceptively simple, and a hallmark of his style is the sure observation of nature in all her moods. *Lakeside Cottages (Pl 9)*, painted in the mid to late 1920s, shows him at his very best. The rugged landscape, with a few cottages and turf stacks by a lake, and a mountain beyond, is a typical Henry composition. Such pictures helped to foster the popular view of the west, and fitted perfectly with the socio-political outlook of the times. Amongst a number of successes in these years was his *West of Ireland Village*, acquired for the prestigious Luxembourg Gallery in Paris, an honour which put a seal of approval on his reputation.

But from the mid-1920s marital difficulties coupled with financial and domestic problems began to affect the quality of Henry's work. Paradoxically, his reputation suffered when, in 1925, two of his paintings, *Connemara* and *A View of Lough Erne*, were reproduced as travel posters for the London Midland and Scottish Railway Company. These were the first of several of his pictures to be reproduced in the 1920s and 1930s. They were enormously popular and were widely distributed to tourist offices in Europe and the United States, helping to create the archetypal image of the west of Ireland. But their success and availability created such a demand for original paintings that Henry ultimately became trapped in his own imagery.

Henceforth Henry lost much of the sparkle of enthusiasm and inventiveness of his earlier period. His compositional technique became stagnant and he turned against any thought of further development. His friend, Arthur Power, with whom he had organised an exhibition of avant-garde

French and British paintings for Dublin Civic Week in 1922, encouraged him to re-trace his steps in Paris and to explore the latest developments in art; but he was not interested. While he continued to exhibit regularly, the quality of his work rarely approached, and never excelled, that of a decade or so earlier.

After he had moved to Dublin, Paul Henry rarely visited the west of Ireland, although he did make occasional forays *31* to Counties Donegal and Antrim. The charcoal drawing entitled *Grand Canal Dock, Ringsend, Dublin* (*Pl 7*) and *Connemara Cottages*, an oil of about 1928, are among his most successful works of that period.

෴

CONTENTMENT IN ENNISKERRY

In 1930, after considerable anguish, Paul and Grace Henry separated. Paul then moved to Carrigoona Cottage, near Enniskerry in County Wicklow, where he settled with Mabel Young, whom he had first met in 1924.

Paul's first exhibition in the United States took place a year before his move to Enniskerry, when his work appeared in a mixed exhibition of contemporary Irish art at the Hackett Gallery in New York. The following year he paid his first visit to America, and held a one-man show at the same venue and also in Boston, where he was treated as a visiting celebrity. On each occasion he exhibited landscapes of the west of Ireland, and others which he had painted on Achill. He was beginning to gather a number of influential friends and patrons amongst the Irish community in New York and, often with their assistance, he held other exhibitions there and in Toronto over the next few years. The Wall Street crash of 1929 and its aftermath, however, severely curtailed his hopes of capitalising on these contacts.

Back in Ireland, Henry's work was still very popular. He exhibited regularly in one-man shows, usually held at Combridge's Gallery in Dublin, and at the Royal Hibernian Academy's annual exhibitions. His compositions then were often based on his earlier sketches, but his visit to County Kerry and the Dingle peninsula in 1934 provided him with fresh subject-matter. *Peat Ditches, Ireland* (*Pl 10*) was almost certainly painted during this visit, and is a good example of his contemporary style. In 1933 he was commissioned by Queen's University, Belfast, to paint a portrait of his elder brother, Robert Mitchell Henry, who was professor of Latin at the university. This oil painting was a rare departure from his usual subject matter, although he had earlier made a number of successful portrait studies in charcoal, such as that of President Cosgrave (1922).

In 1944 Paul Henry suffered a stroke which led to partial

paralysis. His condition deteriorated over time and he became almost totally blind. But he was resilient in spirit and, in the years which followed, despite his failing sight, he wrote a number of short stories and broadcasts, mainly recollections of his early life in the west. He also wrote two autobiographies, *An Irish Portrait,* which was published in 1951, and *Further Reminiscences*, published posthumously in 1973.

Paul Henry and Mabel Young moved to Bray in 1951, and after Grace Henry's death in 1953 they married. The retrospective exhibition of Paul's work, held at Dublin's Ritchie Hendriks Gallery in 1957, was a belated eightieth birthday celebration, and brought him richly deserved approval. He died the following year, on 24 August 1958, and was buried at St Patrick's Church, Enniskerry. Mabel died in 1974.

Despite the repetitiveness of his later work, Paul Henry retained a distinctive manner and, by any standard, must be regarded as one of Ireland's most important landscape painters. In Achill he developed a style perfectly in harmony with his surroundings, and his life there was a reiteration of Synge's visits to the Aran Islands. As did Synge, Henry lived like the people, and recorded a way of life that had never before found expression. In so doing, he became the first Irish painter, working in Ireland, to adopt a true post-impressionist manner, and his efforts in founding the Society of Dublin Painters were of lasting influence on Irish art. He is distinguished from many of his contemporaries in that his work is free from literary references and, in his vision of the landscape, he virtually created a 'school' of painting which others followed.